CENYP

ACN 8382

SANTA CRUZ CITY-COUNTY LIBRARY SYSTEM

0000113917520

D0042182

DISCARDED

J 979.4004 COL

Collins, David R.

Ishi : the last of his
people /
2000.

SANTA CRUZ PUBLIC LIBRARY
Santa Cruz, California

# ISHI
## *The Last of His People*

# ISHI
## *The Last of His People*

**Written by
David R. Collins
and Kristen Bergren**

**Illustrated by Kelly Welch**

MORGAN
REYNOLDS
Incorporated

**Greensboro**

**ISHI: THE LAST OF HIS PEOPLE**

Copyright © 2000 by David R. Collins
and Kristen Bergren

All rights reserved.
This book, or parts thereof, may not be reproduced in any form except
by written consent of the publisher. For information write:
Morgan Reynolds, Inc., 620 S. Elm St., Suite 384
Greensboro, North Carolina 27406 USA

Library of Congress Cataloging-in-Publication Data

Collins, David R.
　　Ishi: the last of his people / written by David R. Collins and Kristen Bergren ;
　　illustrated by Kelly Welch.
　　　p. cm.
　　Includes bibliographical references and index.
　　ISBN 1-883846-54-4 (lib. bdg.)
　　　1. Ishi, d. 1916. 2. Yana Indians--Biography. I. Bergren, Kristen. II. Title.

　E99.Y23 I78 2000
　979.4004'9757--dc21
　[B]

00-024428

Printed in the United States of America
First Edition

*For my husband, Stephen, and sons, Sam and Joe.
I couldn't have written this without your support
and encouragement. All my love, K. B.*

# Contents

Ishi

# Chapter One

## Out of Hiding

A hot sun in a cloudless sky was doing its best to bake the residents of Oroville, California. August was often a warm month and the old timers of the area declared that the August of 1911 would be remembered for its daily battle between heat and humidity. Monday, August 29, promised to be a day like the ten days before it with temperatures keeping local folks fanning their faces and close to their iceboxes. When friends met on street corners or families chattered over dinner, the weather was the main topic of conversation. But, by evening, the residents of Oroville, California, were talking about something far removed from the peak temperatures of the day. There was a stranger in town, a most unusual visitor, and he had managed to capture everyone's attention.

It had all started at the Ward Slaughterhouse on Quincy Road a couple miles out of town when butcher,

Ad Kessler, stopped to wipe the sweat from his face onto his sleeve. The sound of dogs barking outside caught the butcher's attention. As Ad squinted towards the corral, he made out the silhouette of a lone figure. Kessler knew it was not one of his butchers working late that afternoon.

"Who is that?" Ad called out.

No answer came. The hunched outline moved silently forward in the afternoon shadows, then slid to his knees. Grabbing a stick from the ground, Ad advanced.

"Who are you? Speak up."

Still there was no reply. Ad lifted the stick and pushed the weary figure to the ground. Gazing down at the man before him, Ad felt shame race over him. The stranger was thin, his flesh barely covering the bones of his body. He was clearly a Native American, but he did not look like any of the local Digger Tribe. The man looked dazed and confused. His eyes reflected wonder about the place he was in and the man standing above him. Ad reached down and brought the figure into a seated position. The man leaned forward, cupping his hand, and whispering. But the whispers were not words that Ad understood. The butcher summoned other workers to help him guard the stranger. "We got something out here," one of the slaughterhouse butchers telephoned the sheriff, "but we don't know what it is."

Within an hour both Sheriff Webber and the constable of Oroville arrived to take the stranger to jail. Despite the man's weakened condition, they clasped handcuffs on his scrawny wrists.

Once at the Oroville jail, the sheriff sent out for food. The man, wearing a rough canvas shirt that hung to his knees, stuffed food into his mouth like a hungry bear. It was clear he was unaccustomed to doughnuts, first nibbling them suspiciously, then shoving aside a bowl of hot beans to gobble the powdered pastries as fast as he could.

The subject of attention appeared to be about fifty years old, of bony structure, with buckskin rings hanging from his earlobes. The width of his bare feet, almost as wide as they were long, showed plainly that he had never worn moccasins or shoes.

Word of the strange man's appearance traveled fast through the small town. By nightfall, Oroville families were talking about "the wild man" who was being held in the jail. Reporters arrived on the scene. Despite his inability to communicate in English, the stranger made good newspaper copy, and readers were fascinated by his every move and sound. From Columbus's 1492 landing in the Americas, when an estimated 10 million Native Americans lived on the continent, the population had dropped to less than 300,000. Most of these Indians lived on reservations or had been assimilated into the mainstream population. The man confined to the Oroville jail was a curiosity, a living remnant of another place and time.

"The attire of the Indian, his general appearance and his presence here, are strongly indicative of the fact that he belongs to the Deer Creek tribe of wild and uncivilized Indians," wrote a reporter for the *Oroville Register* on August 30, 1911. "These Indians were originally proud and warlike, and their frequent depredations upon the white settlers led to an organized war against them."

Newspaper accounts failed to mention the "depredations" imposed by the white settlers upon the Native Americans following the discovery of California gold in the mid-1800s. Hundreds of Indians were massacred, often in surprise attacks, by invaders hoping to make quick fortunes.

Many readers wanted a look at the human curiosity housed in the Oroville jail. They arrived alone and in groups requesting permission to view the unusual

Ishi arrived emaciated and weak at the Ward Slaughthouse in the summer of 1911.

guest. Countless visitors were taken to the stranger's cell where they peered at the man crouching in the far corner. Many of the visitors yelled out Indian words, hoping to gain a response. None came.

Although he seemed harmless, the stranger was watched closely. Not one recognizable word came from his mouth. He was, however, interested in the process of writing. Handed a pencil himself, he held it, examined it, then set it down. Offered a cigarette, he showed recognition, but he did not smoke it.

Hoping to learn how the man had found his way to Oroville, authorities returned him to the slaughterhouse on Quincy Road. He seemed to know what his hosts wanted, and with sweeping arm motions, pantomine, and strange language, he explained the journey that had brought him to the Ward Slaughterhouse. The listeners strained to make sense of the animated figure before them.

The stranger had come from the northwest, leaving his home at the base of Mount Lassen in the Cascade Mountains with three companions. The listeners recognized the word *mahala* as "mother." Two of his friends had drowned in a stream they tried to cross. Although the bodies had been washed away, the man had dug graves and held a burial ceremony. When he returned to his mother, she was near death. After holding her to keep her warm, she died in his arms. Once again he had dug a grave and buried the remains of his last family member while chanting a song for the dead. He traveled alone until he reached the slaughterhouse where he had stopped in hopes of finding food. Convinced he was telling the truth, the authorities took him back to the Oroville jail.

The problem remained of what to do with the stranger. At most, he was guilty of trespassing, yet the owners of the Ward Slaughterhouse had no interest in pressing charges. Otherwise, he had commited no crime, unless being "the last member of a tribe long believed to be extinct," as the *San Francisco Examiner* put it, was against the law.

But clearly something had to be done. In Washington, President William Howard Taft had been informed of the situation by the United States Bureau of Indian Affairs. The chief executive put any decision-making back into the hands of the agency. "Do the right thing with this man," Taft ordered. "He is a part of our country's history." A national election was scheduled for November, and Taft was busy trying to hold on to the presidency against former president, Theodore Roosevelt, and an eloquent challenger named Woodrow Wilson. Taft wanted to do nothing that would upset any voters, therefore, he kept out of the drama unfolding in California.

However, two men in California took a special interest in the mysterious Native American housed in the Oroville jail. Alfred Kroeber, the first professor of anthropology at the University of California at Berkeley, and his teaching colleague, Thomas Waterman, had been studying California Native Americans for years. They had traveled all over the state searching for Native Americans to interview. Their subjects seldom wished to talk about the past, their tribes, or their cultures. Kroeber wanted to find Native Americans who were free of the modern world and its way of living. "A record of their traits and habits, preserved from purely aboriginal times, into the twentieth century, would be a rich mine to the anthropologist of the future," said Kroeber. The discovery of a non-assimilated Indian excited him. Who was this "wild man" and of what tribe?

Three years before, in 1908, surveyors near Oroville had stumbled onto a group of Native Americans, hiding out in the brush near Deer Creek some forty miles north. The startled people had fled, leaving behind weapons and belongings. An examination revealed the objects were Yahi, derived from the Yana tribe. The Yahi were largely wiped out by settlers in the massacres of the 1860s. Those who survived had hidden themselves in mountain caves and area woodlands for forty years. Could the stranger of Oroville be the last of the Yahi?

Professor Kroeber called the Bureau of Indian Affairs and expressed his interest in the stranger. Then he called the sheriff of Oroville. Kroeber asked if his assistant, Thomas Waterman, could come to visit the guest housed in the town jail. If so, Waterman would catch the next train. Eager to put the stranger in the right hands, Sheriff Webber agreed.

When Waterman came to meet the Indian, the professor brought a list of old Native American words, many from the Yana tribe. As Waterman read the words, the man nodded. Most of the words were familiar to him.

Waterman observed the man's hair was burned close to the scalp. The professor knew that many Indians did this when they had lost loved ones. Whether he had suffered a recent loss or whether the man had burned his hair in honor of his people who had died years before, no one knew. Waterman sensed this man feared he might be killed too.

Sam Batwi, one of the oldest remaining Yana, arrived from Redding, California. Professor Kroeber and Professor Waterman hoped he might be able to communicate with the stranger. At first Batwi seemed to frighten the captive more than the white men. But soon the two men relaxed. Although they seemed to know each other's words, communication was ragged. Batwi confirmed that his new acquaintance was indeed a Yahi, one of the Deer Creek tribe, but that he did not know his dialect.

Eager to have Professor Kroeber meet his new friend, Waterman arranged for the Indian to travel by train to the Berkeley campus in San Francisco. He could stay at the museum there. Sheriff Webber was glad to see his visitor go. The lawman was eager to have Oroville return to its former sleepy state. Not since the days of the Gold Rush from which the town was born had Oroville been so bustling. "The Indian wasn't any trouble at all," said the exhausted Webber. "It was just that people showed up at all hours to take a peek at him."

The stranger was outfitted with a new set of clothes for the journey to San Francisco. He seemed comfortable enough in a gray suit, a cutaway coat and a straw hat. He carried the pair of shoes that had been purchased for him under his arm. As Waterman and the "Wild Man of Oroville" walked from the jail to the train station, many sets of eyes watched from behind windows and fences.

Once on the train, the stranger appeared nervous at the sounds of the engine and the hissing steam, and he clasped the chair rails. His hold did not ease up as the train slid along the track. Onlookers stared openly at him, and he returned their gazes with alert eyes and a slight smile.

When Professor Kroeber and the stranger met, an immediate bond formed between the two men. "He was so gentle," Kroeber wrote in his journal. "He was curious about everything, his eyes looking everywhere. I had the sense we were embarking on a wonderful journey. We had no map to follow for our odyssey, only a desire to know and understand each other's worlds."

# Chapter Two

---

## Two Worlds Meet

If Professor Kroeber and Professor Waterman believed the stranger they welcomed into their lives would be theirs alone, they were in for a big surprise. The mysterious stranger who entered the slaughterhouse outside Oroville that August day meant something special to reporters too. He was big news, a feature attraction to readers across the country. The accountant in Seattle, the housewife in Moline, the teacher in Atlanta—each of them wanted to know more about this man from a bygone world. The reporters wanted a name for him too. Indeed, they demanded that he have a name.

So, too, did the museum people with whom Kroeber worked. After all, the stranger was living at the University of California Museum of Anthropology in Berkeley. Many in the building saw him often, passing him as they came and went and sharing meals with him. Even Waterman felt he should have a name. "We can't go on calling him 'Hey there!' " exclaimed the professor.

Sam Batwi simply called the stranger John. Professor Kroeber rejected that name, feeling it was "far too ordinary a label to affix to such an extraordinary man." It was also an English name, and hardly suitable for a full-blooded American Indian.

It was perfectly clear that the stranger himself did not care at all what he was called. It was considered rude among Native American tribes to ask anyone's name, at least until a bond of friendship had been established. There was also an old belief that to volunteer one's name was vain and a violation of spiritual law.

Finally, Kroeber gave in to the requests. "Very well. He shall be called Ishi," declared the professor. "It is a word meaning 'Man' in the Yahi Tribe from which he has come."

Ishi. It was a curious name. It seemed to arouse even more curiosity among the public. Newspaper readers could not get enough of the "untamed savage of a past world," as one reporter wrote. Ishi was the topic of conversation at dinner tables, gossip at bridge clubs, and animated chatter at workplaces. People across the country seemed bored with the 1912 presidential run. The incumbent, President Taft, joked about being "the second most talked about man in America, next to that Indian out West."

As for Ishi, he seemed confused by all the attention. Often his eyebrows arched, expressing his wonder and amazement. Each day he met with Professor Kroeber, using hand and arm motions to try to share his thoughts. The mood was friendly. Yet, at times, Kroeber displayed frustration when it was clear he was not getting through to Ishi. "It is my failing, not his," the professor wrote in his journal.

When not being questioned and interviewed, Ishi made himself at home in the museum. He wandered about, picking up artifacts and examining them closely. With some of the Native American pieces, his face seemed to show recognition. Bows and arrows captured his interest the most. The Yahi were known to be fine hunters. Ishi handled the weapons with sure hands, hands that had probably one day stretched sinew string to lace a juniper wood bow. Other artifacts in the Native American section of the museum he seemed to be observing for the first time.

Professor Kroeber welcomed others to visit with Ishi. Indians came from miles to "talk" with him, while scholars well versed in Native American languages came too. None of the visitors could understand his speech, but he pantomimed his main ideas. He could not understand his visitors' words, yet he responded with warmth and appreciation to their efforts.

"He is without trace or taint of civilization," wrote one reporter in the September 6, 1911 issue of the *San Francisco Call,* "but he is learning fast and seems to enjoy the process."

Eating was one of the "processes" Ishi enjoyed most. Ever since his discovery in the Oroville slaughterhouse, he ate well. He accepted the use of a knife, fork, and spoon quickly, often smiling between bites. Ishi gained forty pounds in three months, and his five-foot-eight-inch frame displayed well formed muscles with little fat. His hair was thick and dark as coal. His alert eyes were dark, and thick eyelashes extended over them. He had a straight nose, and a long chin. He had long, narrow hands, and his fingers were slender. His palms were soft, showing evidence of little manual labor. His ears and nose were pierced, a sign of religious belief according to Sam Batwi. Batwi explained that the piercing expressed the hope of going to a good place after death. In Ishi's ears hung sinews, or animal tendons. He showed no interest in shaving, preferring to pluck his whiskers upon their arrival.

Ishi was usually cooperative and friendly at the museum. One afternoon, when photographers asked him to slip out of his overalls and into animal skins so they could take his picture, he refused. With considerable coaxing, he was persuaded to roll his pants up to the knee so the skins could hang over them. The photographers wanted to present as much of their idea of a Native American's appearance as they could. Ishi's compressed lips and dilated nostrils showed his displeasure. A nervous Thomas Waterman leaned over to Sam Batwi. "Tell him, Batwi, white man just play," he whispered. Sam Batwi delivered the message to Ishi, who seemed to relax a bit. But as soon as the picture-taking session ended, the skins were discarded.

Not long after his arrival in Berkeley, a couple of newspaper reporters persuaded Ishi to attend a vaudeville show at the Orpheum Theatre. Vaudeville featured a variety of singing, dancing, and comedy acts. Kroeber was hesitant about the idea, knowing Ishi would probably not understand the performance at all. But Ishi seemed willing to attend, so Kroeber and

Ishi and Dr. Alfred Kroeber became friends at the University of California at Berkeley.

Waterman tagged along, more as observers than anything else. Sam Batwi also joined the group.

Seated in the box seats that overlooked the audience, Ishi seemed more interested in the people on the floor than on the stage. Vaudeville attracted the city's elite, and when they attended such affairs, most enjoyed showing off their finest clothes and jewelry. Sequins sparkled on ladies' hats and men wore glittering diamond stickpins. Hoping to catch the visiting Native American's attention, one of the performers brought Ishi into his act.

"And sitting in the box you see," the actor declared, "the Indian from the Universitee...."

The crowd gazed upward and applauded. Not understanding what was happening, Ishi smiled and applauded too. Throughout the performance, Ishi's expression did not change. On the way home, he chose to talk in broken English about the audience rather than the show itself.

Ishi enjoyed taking automobile rides. Scenic San Francisco offered miles of hillside streets, and he gazed with awe from an open-roofed vehicle at the tall and sprawling buildings. Ishi's eyes widened at the thousands of people enjoying the ocean beaches of Golden Gate Park when they visited there one afternoon. He had never seen so many people at once!

"*Hansi saltu!*" he exclaimed.

"Yes, many white people," Kroeber agreed.

Later, when the automobile rolled over a little-used road, a nearby flock of quail lifted into the air. Ishi stood up in the car, watching their every move.

One morning an agent from the Bureau of Indian Affairs visited the museum. The government representative had plans for Ishi. "You are free to go back to Deer Creek," C. E. Kelsey told Ishi. "Or perhaps you might wish to go to a reservation to be with your people." The agent turned to Professor Kroeber. "It might be his wish that the Indian be with his own people."

Kroeber was puzzled. "His own people? His own people are dead," the professor replied, "many of them killed by white men, I'm afraid. We have made a home for him here. He seems to like us—and we like him."

The representative's eyes widened. "But he can't stay here forever. Sooner or later, he has to make a way for himself in the world. He must learn to live with people, to work, to earn a living—"

"Earn a living?" Kroeber interrupted. "Why, he is doing that now. I have hired him to work here as a museum helper. He is being paid ten dollars a week. I might add that Ishi handles a broom, a mop, and a duster with greater energy and enthusiasm than most of our other staff. He also keeps his room sparkling clean!"

"Hmmmm...." the representative rose from his chair. He thought Ishi would have welcomed the chance to rejoin a Native American tribe. "Well, please let the man know that anytime he wishes, he may be placed on a reservation. The United States government wants our Native Americans to receive proper treatment."

"Oh, like they have received in the past?" the professor answered curtly. "I shall inform Ishi of that."

Kroeber showed the representative out and then went to Ishi's room. He struggled with the Yahi words he knew, hoping to convey the representative's offer clearly.

Ishi nodded, fumbling for the right words too. "I should like to live here," Ishi said, in his Yahi tongue. "I should like to live here and when I die, I should like to die here."

Professor Kroeber smiled. He had hoped his new friend felt that way.

# Chapter Three

## The Arrow

*Whirrr-clap. Whirrr-clap.*

"What is that sound?" thought Professor Kroeber. *Whirrr-clap.* It seemed to come out of Ishi's small room and echoed off the tall ceiling of the museum hallway. Professor Kroeber quickened his step. He couldn't imagine what was making that strange noise until he stepped into Ishi's doorway.

There Ishi stood by the window with the lower edge of the shade in his hand. He let it go and the shade snapped quickly to the top. Ishi gave Professor Kroeber a look of delight and puzzlement.

"Where it go, Chiep?" asked Ishi.

"Chiep" was Ishi's name for Kroeber. He had been told that Professor Kroeber was in charge of the museum, like a chief in charge of his people. Ishi had difficulty pronouncing "f" so "Chief" became "Chiep." He also attached "tee" to the ends of new words, so that he called Professor Waterman, "Waterman-tee."

Ishi's question about the window shade seemed to require a simple but thoughtful answer. While gesturing Kroeber said, "It rolls up into itself." Ishi nodded with a quizzical look at the shade and smiled.

Ishi had been introduced to many modern inventions since he came to the museum. But the ones that seemed to impress and mystify him the most were the common, everyday items like the window shade. Once, when he was taken to a viewpoint overlooking the city where he could see thousands of homes, Ishi appeared unimpressed. Yet when someone handed him a tiny penny whistle, he blew into it and became totally captivated by the gift.

"Please, Ishi, sit down," said Kroeber as he pointed to the chair by the window. "What shall we learn about each other today?" he asked, more to himself than to his new friend. Kroeber was sensitive to the etiquette and customs of the California Indian cultures. He knew it would take time before he would learn of Ishi's painful past. Of course, the first obstacle was to better understand each other's languages and then hopefully they would better understand each other's hearts.

Ishi stared out the window over the tree tops and

the strange new buildings as if searching for something familiar. The sky was familiar. The blue sky and
the white clouds took him back to his home in the
canyon at Deer Creek. The years drifted away and he
was a boy again. Ishi told Kroeber about his memories.

Young Ishi leaned on the smooth sun-warmed
boulder and gazed at the animal shaped clouds in the
brilliant blue sky. Ishi's elder uncle held his spear
high as he peered in the canyon's clear water for
salmon. There were few men of his tribe left who
could provide food for them. The *saltu,* or white
settlers, had taken their lands, had hunted their deer,
and had killed his people. The white men had been
his people's enemy as long as Ishi could remember.
They came to search the Yahi's streams for the golden
rocks that shone in the sun. Ishi wondered if the stones
had an evil spirit who told the *saltu* to destroy the
Yahi.

Ishi moved off the boulder and found the trail to
the juniper trees. He was in search of a branch to make
a hunting bow. Ishi looked for a limb that was strong
and straight. When he was satisfied that he had found
a bow branch, he pulled out his tools from his leather
pouch. He would not chop down the limb. The chopping

sound would let the *saltu* know the Yahi were nearby. Instead Ishi knew he had to take the branch off and leave the juniper looking unharmed. With his sharpened stone Ishi made a small cut and bent the branch back and forth. He repeated this procedure until the branch silently broke off the tree without leaving a mark.

Ishi followed the path through the underbrush that led to the Yahi camp. He knew he could leave no footprints on the trail to his home. Ishi covered his tracks with leaves, jumped from boulder to boulder, and walked in the stream to keep the existence of his people hidden from the white intruders. Hunger growled inside of him. He looked forward to the salmon, acorn mush, and berries that his mother would have for him at the family home. Although he now slept in the men's house, or *watugurwa*, the family still took their meals together.

Night pushed day aside; the evening shadows spread in the forests and canyonlands. Ishi quickened his step so he could reach home before darkness cloaked the area.

Ishi's tribe of Yahi built their village between a creek bank and the flat ledges of a canyon. The people knew how to remain unseen among the brush, hunting wildlife and fishing Deer and Mill Creeks that spilled across their homeland.

It had not always been that way. Long before Ishi was born, the Yahi freely roamed the rich California foothills, living off what nature provided. It was only after gold was found at a mill along the Sacramento River in 1848 that the white settlers poured in, seeking instant fortunes from the waters. They chased away the small Indian tribes, sending them into hiding.

A fire crackled and lit the faces of Ishi's Grandfather and Elder Uncle. Ishi took his place beside them and worked on his hunting bow, tying the deer sinew around the juniper branch. As was the custom, Ishi waited until there was quiet between the older men before he spoke.

"Grandfather and Elder Uncle, I am making my hunting bow. I am doing as you have taught me. I found a branch that was straight so my arrows would fly fast and strong. The bow will bend only in my strong hands. You have been my teachers since the white skins killed my father at our home in Three Knolls."

The boy stopped, looking down. Then he gazed up again.

"When my hunting bow is finished, I want to go with you to help protect our people from our enemy."

Elder Uncle looked at his nephew with pain in his heart. Ishi was his younger brother's only child. Ishi had never known the freedom of childhood, the days of running through rainbow colored meadows and swimming in the snow-fed mountain streams without fear of the *saltu*. When Ishi's father and brother were young, their days were filled with adventure and dreams. Ishi had known seclusion and nightmares. He hardly knew what it was to swim in nearby creeks or to run with the sun's warm rays on his brown, smooth skin without fear.

Grandfather laid his hand on Ishi's head and stroked his hair. His grandson had only lived through eight winters but the boy had lived a lifetime of sorrows. "Ishi," he spoke softly, "when the *saltu* first came to our valley, the young hunters would hide on the ridge and shower them with arrows. But soon there were too many white skins and too many firesticks. We could no longer fight. Our people had to learn to hide from the enemy."

The old man paused a moment. It was hard to remember and share sad memories. But he knew it was necessary.

As a boy, Ishi learned how to make hunting bows from juniper and sinew.

"Your father taught our people to disappear into the shadows of dark caves," Grandfather continued. "He showed us how to cover ourselves under a blanket of leaves or behind a bush of poison oak or spring manzanita. He showed us how the silvery wall of a waterfall could hide our people from the *saltu*'s firesticks. He taught the young hunters how to slip into the icy mountain waters and silently come to the edge for only a short breath of lifegiving air."

"I like to hear of my brave father. Did he kill many *saltu*?" asked Ishi.

"Your father knew he could not kill enough of the *saltu*. So he led the white skins away from our camps. He made fires and left trails to fool them. One time he had them chasing him for more than two moons," Grandfather said with great pride. "It is sad that you could not have grown up with him beside you. He was a brave and noble Yahi, caring and kind. I wish that he were here to guide you rather than for me to tell you stories. But my prayer is that his spirit is within you, that you be strong as he was strong."

Elder Uncle looked at his young nephew and spoke. "It was soon after that, when your father fooled the white man and led them astray, that other white skins found our homes at Three Knolls. Your father was killed trying to protect his family. Giving his life gave time for you and your mother to hide."

Ishi was silent now as the words of Grandfather and Elder Uncle settled in his heart. He longed for his father. Ishi watched the fire crackle and spit sparks into the night air as the smoke lifted the small glowing embers toward the stars. His thoughts traveled back to his home in Three Knolls Village. He could remember only patches of time from when he was a small boy, but listening to his elders while watching the flames dance and smelling the burning juniper branches seem to awaken memories of that terrifying day.

Ishi had been little enough to be curled up into his mother's lap. She held him tight as the first gun shots broke the silence in their small home. Ishi's father signaled to his wife to follow him. He tried to shield them with his body as they ran to the stream with the other frightened Yahi. The white men's guns sounded like sharp thunder splitting the sky. Gun smoke filled the air along with the screams and cries of the defenseless Yahi. Ishi's father helped his wife and son into the rushing stream. His mother cried as they helplessly slid downstream in the blood-stained mountain water. The dead bodies of their people swirled in the current and crashed into boulders. One of them was Ishi's father.

Elder Uncle went into the *watugurwa*. When he returned, he handed Ishi an arrow and quietly spoke to him again. "Ishi, when the sun rises you will hunt with me, not for our enemy but for food. There are too many *saltu* to fight. The hunting bow gives us life by giving us food, not by killing the white men. You must stay strong to make the hunting bows. One day I will be too old and weak to bend the sturdy juniper branch as I have taught you. You must stay strong to protect your family from hunger. Your father would be proud of his son. He would want you to have this, his last arrow. I have saved it for the time when you would become a *wanasi*.

Ishi tenderly took the arrow and touched the smooth hazelwood shaft that his father had made. It was a perfect size and shape. How swiftly it would cut through the air to find its target.

The fire had burned down to ashes. Dark clouds hid the stars as Ishi and his elders entered the *watugurwa*. Ishi pulled the rabbitskin blanket on top of him. He grasped his arrow and held it close to him. He slept and dreamed of his father.

# Chapter Four

## Wanasi

Early morning light seeped through the walls of the *watugurwa* and awoke Ishi. He reached for his father's arrow to be sure it was still there. As his fingers touched the obsidian arrowhead, Ishi felt his father's spirit come to him. He carefully put the arrow in his otterskin quiver. Ishi carried the arrow so his father's spirit would stay with him. On this day he would become a *wanasi*, a hunter.

Ishi joined his uncle in the cool morning air. Before the hunt they cleansed themselves of the smells of smoke and cooked food in the creek below the steep, rough walls of the canyon. A narrow path led them through the tall trees that shaded their small village to the cliff. With ropes made of milkweed fiber they lowered themselves safely down the canyon walls. The Yahi preferred to use the ropes. It was faster to repel down the rocky sides than to walk the treacherous trail. Also, by lowering a basket, they could bring up a catch of fish or water with little effort.

The preparation continued after their bath. Elder Uncle and Ishi made small cuts on their arms and legs with a stone. The cuts were to strengthen them for the long day of hunting.

"Ishi, as you learn to be a *wanasi*," said Elder Uncle, "be ready to move silently through the brush in search of your prey. Open your senses to the sights, sounds, and smells that will allow you to know the animal's presence."

Ishi nodded solemnly. Clad in their buckskin breech-cloths and with their bows and quivers hanging from their backs, Elder Uncle and Ishi walked into the deep canyon. It was dawn and the pink sunrise reflected on the rugged walls. Spring greenery spilled out of crevices and pine trees jutted precariously from the ledges overhead. The scent of bay trees filled the air along with the cries of circling falcons. Ishi felt all his senses awaken.

A meadow of tall grass hid them as they headed towards the woods. Elder Uncle preferred luring an animal close to him, instead of stalking and chasing his prey. He chose a pile of boulders on the edge of the clearing for them to hide behind.

Ishi watched Elder Uncle intently as he readied himself for the hunt. Drawing back his bow, he tested the sinew string. It was not tight enough. Elder Uncle readjusted the brace and told Ishi to do the same to his bow.

With his uncle watching him, Ishi held his hunting bow in his left hand and with all his strength he drew back the taunt string with his right until it reached his chin. Elder Uncle gave Ishi a nod of approval and put three arrows under his right arm. Ishi did the same but was careful not to choose his father's arrow. Elder Uncle took a mandrone leaf and folded it in between his lips and made a sucking noise to imitate the whimpering of a fawn. The sound might bring a doe out in search of her fawn. Now it was time to wait.

Elder Uncle and Ishi crouched down behind the rocks to conceal themselves from any animal that might come into the clearing. Ishi, remembering his uncle's advice, kept all senses alert. If they were able to keep concealed from their quarry, Ishi and his uncle still might have to wait hours for the unsuspecting animal to come within shooting distance. Elder Uncle felt it was better to be patient and stay in one spot, rather than hunting in many places in one day.

The day was still early but the canyon was becoming warmer. Deer and rabbit were cautiously making their way through the meadow, grazing when they felt confident to stop and nibble the sweet grasses and wildflowers. As a rabbit came closer to their hiding spot, Ishi positioned himself with his bow and arrow. Drawing the arrow back as far as his young arms would allow and keeping his bow still, Ishi released the arrow. It sliced the morning air without a sound and slipped past the unsuspecting animal. Ishi couldn't look at his uncle, afraid to see the disappointment in his eyes. Elder Uncle laid his hand on Ishi's shoulder. "Try again, *wanasi*," he whispered.

Ishi reached into his quiver. This time he took out his father's arrow. The boy stared at it, his face filled with hope. Again he drew, aimed, and this time the arrow found its mark. Elder Uncle put his hand on Ishi's shoulder and smiled.

Moments later Ishi and his uncle knelt over the fallen rabbit and gave thanks for the gifts their family would receive from it. Its meat would help take away their hunger and its fur would help protect them from winter's cold. The young boy carefully pulled the arrow from the rabbit's body and also gave thanks to his father's spirit for helping him to become a *wanasi* this day. They buried the carcass in a cache by the mound of boulders. They would dig it up to take home when they finished hunting.

Ishi was enjoying this time spent with his uncle. Elder Uncle told him stories about when he was a young *wanasi*. Then, Yahi hunted freely, never fearful of an attack from the white settlers. Ishi was learning much from this man who had been like a father to him. The hunting had been good, four rabbits and one deer falling before their arrows. It would take several days to carry back the meat they had buried. They journeyed further into the canyon heading towards Green Cave. Elder Uncle traced the past with his words, remembering slowly many moons ago.

As the settlers had invaded their world, the Yahi found ways to hide themselves from their enemy. By dividing their tribe into small groups, the Yahi were better able to conceal their existence from the *saltu*. Elder Uncle wanted to go to Green Cave and talk to the old ones hiding there.

The two hunters, man and boy, found a small cave for shelter as night slowly descended into the canyon. A crimson sunset outlined the rugged ledges and soon darkness fell. Sparrows and bats flew in the dark canyon. Exhausted from their day, the man and boy welcomed sleep.

"*Wanasi, wanasi*, we must leave soon," Elder Uncle whispered to Ishi as the first traces of morning sun appeared. They gathered their quivers and bows and arrows and followed the narrow trail that led into the dense forest. The trees and thickets of scrub oak would give them cover from the settlers as they journeyed to Green Cave.

Even in the most remote area of this canyon country, a few whites had tried to settle. They constructed small crude cabins in various parts of the wilderness. Some were searching for gold. Some were looking for land to ranch. They brought small herds of cattle to graze on the vegetation that bordered the impenetrable forests. Stray steers often became prey for the hungry Yahi.

Elder Uncle bent down to touch a dark brown spot on the ground. Ishi noticed that there were other brown spots that stained the leaves on the underbrush. They followed the markings until they found the source. A mutilated carcass of a steer laid strewn about in several large pieces. One had a broken arrow sticking out of it.

"Uncle, what has happened here? This is not the way of our people to leave animals they hunt," said Ishi, staring at the bloody remains.

Ishi hunted for deer and rabbit to help feed his family.

Fearing for their safety, Elder Uncle did not answer right away but motioned for Ishi to follow him into the shadows of the underbrush.

"*Wanasi*, I'm afraid our people were found while preparing the animal to be taken back to their home. They were probably forced to disappear into the forest as we have done to protect ourselves from the *saltu*," Elder Uncle told Ishi. "At Green Cave, the old ones will tell us what has happened."

Ishi remembered his mother telling him about Green Cave. Clear spring water snaked its way throughout the cave and fed the ferns that grew there. Unlike the small crevice in the canyon where they had slept the night before, this was a large cave. It was tall enough to stand in and deep enough to have a small fire without the smoke being seen from the outside. Ishi was eager to see this wondrous home of his people, many who had witnessed the passing of many moons.

The path that led to the opening was only wide enough for small animals to follow and the sure-footed Yahi. Cautiously, Elder Uncle led the way. He became aware of the silence as they approached the opening. Then he became aware of the smell. His senses awakened and brought memories back of

Three Knolls where his brother and many others were murdered and to Dry Cave where other Yahi hunters were scalped.

Elder Uncle called out to the Old Ones, but he was answered only with silence. He told Ishi to stay on the trail as he entered the cave. As Elder Uncle's eyes became accustomed to the dim light, he saw the work of the *saltu*. Everyone, the Old Ones, women, children, and *wanasi*, had been massacred.

Elder Uncle heard Ishi call out to him, but he could not answer. He was filled with anger and grief. Ishi heard his uncle's sorrowful yell and ran to him.

# Chapter Five

## Fight for Survival

At the time of the harvest, the *watugurwa*, the mothers' house, and the small storehouses were ready for the bitter weather ahead. The Yahi stacked wood behind their houses to use during the deadly storms. The storehouses were filled with baskets of white and black acorns, dried deer meat, smoked salmon, dried berries, nuts, and seeds.

Besides food, the Yahi also collected items they needed for health and winter work. The men had a supply of stone and obsidian for arrowheads. Pelts of skunk, squirrel, and rabbit were bundled, ready to be sewn into blankets and clothes. The women would weave and decorate baskets with dried grasses and dye. Then they would coat the baskets with sticky pine resin to enable them to hold water. They kept roots to make poultices and to wash hair. Herbs with healing powers were used for teas.

As winter passed the tribe was kept busy working. The villagers lived quietly, the older ones often sharing stories of times past with the younger. At one time there were 125,000 Native Americans living in California with some forty major groups, including the Yana. Five hundred different tribes existed, the Yahi just one of many. Ishi loved hearing the stories of these times. Now the Yahi was a band of hideaways, living the dark months tucked away in the shadow of the mountains.

Each day the baskets slowly emptied. Little by little, the supplies were shortened, but soon, the weather began to warm. It was time to find food.

Two springs had passed since the Green Cave massacre, and Ishi's tribe now numbered less than twenty. Afraid of another ambush, they hunted and searched for food together in small groups. The women and children searched the forest and river banks for roots and herbs. Ishi and the other *wanasi* ventured into the forest, setting snares in the hope of killing a rabbit, or if they were lucky, a small deer.

Because so few deer ventured near the Yahi settlement, the Indians sometimes were forced to steal a steer that belonged to the *saltu*. One day, a rancher missing several heads of cattle organized a search for the guilty Yahi. The posse came upon a small group of Yahi women, children, and one old man heading downstream with their baskets of roots and bark.

The posse ducked behind trees and waited for the Indians to approach. As the group wading in the cold water grew near, two of the white men jumped from their hiding places waving and shouting for the women and children to get down into the river. One woman holding a baby grabbed the arm of a young girl who tried to run away, fearing she would be shot. The posse began to fire. The women and children threw themselves down into the clear water or on nearby rocks.

The old man attemped to run to the bank of the river and find cover. One of the *saltu* took careful aim and fired. The report echoed through the valley. The women in the river could smell the powder filtering through the morning air. He fired again and again. The fourth shot brought the old Indian down. Most of the group had by this time escaped into the woods along the river bank. The woman who had stopped the young girl from running and her child were captured.

Ishi and the other *wanasi* heard the gun shots from the forest. Without a word to one another, they slipped through the underbrush, silently making their way to the village where they met the frightened women and children returning from the ambush. Ishi listened to the elders advice. They must try to recover the woman and her child who were taken hostage at the ambush. The elders decided to offer the *saltu* gifts in exchange for the two lives.

The new moon helped protect Ishi and the others as they walked silently to the white man's cabin. Ishi's mother put her arm around her son as they stood at the edge of a small clearing and watched Grandfather, Elder Uncle, and three other *wanasi* line up ceremoniously and present the *saltu* with their hunting bows.

The bows were made of mountain juniper and had been shaped and seasoned by Yahi artisans. Each bow was made to fit the body and hands of its creator. With great patience, the ends had been curved using heated stones to shape the arch, then bent further so the deer sinew string could be attached. Until Ishi grew to manhood, these few men were the last of the Yahi who had the strength to bend the juniper stave into bows.

Ishi watched as the white man signalled for the Yahi to follow him. Ishi was nervous, wondering if the *saltu* were trying to play a trick on them. He watched his elders walk to another cabin where two white men stood guard.

As a guard opened the door, Ishi could see the woman. She was sitting on the floor of the cabin, cradling her small child in her arms. There was talk among the *saltu,* but they did not let the two captives go.

The rancher whose steer had been killed was not at home, and the *saltu* in charge of the hostages could not make an exchange without his consent. Elder Uncle returned to the forest to tell the others, and they all settled in to wait.

Ishi sat for a long time in the dark shadows beneath the pine boughs, shifting in his mother's embrace. A sound came from the cabin. Ishi saw three men emerge from inside. They had been part of the posse that day.

The men sauntered over to the corral. Ishi's mother held him closer to her as they watched a guard swing a long rope over the limb of an oak near the corral. Ishi's mother gasped with fright. She gathered Ishi up and with the others ran into the dark forest. The white settlers had hung many Yahi in the past. The threat forced Ishi and the last survivors of the great Yahi nation to disappear from the rest of the world.

Ishi was eight years old when he entered into a life of seclusion. For twelve years in the canyon there was no more evidence of the Yahi. No cattle or horses were stolen. There were no sightings of *wanasi* or signs of campfires. Ishi learned to move in silence along the banks of rivers or in the forest. The boy often paused to listen for the sounds around him. He knew every animal, every bird. He knew their smells and how they moved.

As the years went by, Ishi grew taller and stronger. He no longer had to look up into the face of Grandfather or Elder Uncle. He held his bow firmly and sent precise arrows flying. He swam and fished with a harpoon in Deer Creek.

When Grandfather passed into the Land of the Dead, Ishi mourned. The young *wanasi* hoped Grandfather would join his father and send their spirits, so full of strength and wisdom, to him so that he might help the remaining Yahi.

Starvation eventually broke the interlude of solitude for Ishi and the four remaining Yahi. Roads and ranches were bringing more people ever closer to the discovery of their homes, making it difficult to hunt and gather foods. Ishi, in his desperation, resorted to raiding cabins with his female cousin. They moved swiftly, the two of them, entering a homestead and departing with what flour, vegetables, and clothes they could carry.

One night they approached a roughly hewn log cabin shaded by a grove of oak trees. Ishi motioned to his cousin to follow him to the back of the cabin. With his stone blade, he pried the window from its frame and they quickly climbed in. Ishi gathered a sack of flour and some potatoes. His cousin took the owner's jacket off a hook by the door. Then they heard a gunshot explode nearby. They fled through the window, but the owner was there waiting for them. Ishi and his cousin backed against the wall, staring at the man fearfully and waiting for his next move. He put down his gun. The man talked to them in a calm voice and then motioned for them to take the things they had gathered. Puzzled and relieved, Ishi and his cousin fled.

That evening, as they ate acorn mush from woven baskets, Ishi and his cousin shared their story with the others. Ishi told how the settler had bravely laid down his weapon. Ishi's cousin told how he spoke to them quietly and motioned for them to take the food and clothes. These were signs of a good heart. How could they show him there was kindness in their hearts also?

The next morning, mist sank deep into the canyon giving Ishi and his cousin a protective cover as they returned to the cabin. Again Ishi pried open the single window, but this time they left gifts for the kind settler. When the man returned he opened the door to his small home and saw two baskets on his wooden table. He carried one outside to look at it in the sunlight. His fingers followed the milkweed fiber design as it circled endlessly throughout the hemp strands. The man shaded his eyes as he looked up into the rugged stone walls searching for its maker. Seeing only the remote canyon valley, he shook his head, smiled, and carried his gift back inside.

Rumors spread that there were malicious Indians raiding cabins throughout the area. None were ever spotted, except for by the friendly *saltu* who had been repaid for his kindness. Once, a man named Polk saw a couple of figures in the brush at Speegle Ranch. Polk watched as the figures disappeared into the brush. Efforts to track them were futile, but with each retelling, the story became more embellished until it was believed that a band of Indians had chased Polk for miles before he gave up his supply of cornmeal and jerky. Rumors like this greeted the 100,000 new settlers arriving in California in the year 1906.

Ishi's world was growing smaller. There were only four of his people left: himself, his mother, cousin and Elder Uncle. Ishi's mother and Elder Uncle were too old to go far from camp. Ishi and his cousin would fish and pick berries for them to eat. Sometimes they would hunt squirrels and rabbits with a snare or Ishi's bow. They made every move with care—a snapping twig might alert the *saltu*.

Ishi stood midstream on a boulder with his harpoon searching for salmon as the mountain river rushed over layers of rock. The roar of the water filled the cool evening air and covered the sound of the two men walking upstream. Ishi looked up from the water and was startled to see two white men standing as still as stone staring at him. Fear and surprise filled them all. No one spoke for a long moment. Finally, Ishi yelled angrily, motioning for the men to go away. The frightened men quickly obliged.

Ishi followed the animal trail that led to the hideout, a group of three small huts where they kept clothing and tools. Not far away was a cave, a second home in case of sudden attack. Tall trees hid the camp from view. Ishi had woven together strips of cedar bark to cover the cave entrance.

"My family," Ishi quickly told the others, "our

home is endangered of being discovered by our enemy. Two *saltu* stood on the shore of Deer Creek as I was fishing for salmon. I yelled to them to go away. They ran back downstream towards their camp. Tomorrow will bring more *saltu* to our river and then to our village."

Ishi spoke to his cousin. "We must have a plan to help the old ones hide from the white intruders." She looked at Ishi bravely and nodded in agreement.

Seeking refuge in the canyon would be difficult. If the intruders returned, Ishi's cousin would help Elder Uncle cross the treacherous waters of Deer Creek. Ishi's mother was weak and unable to walk. Ishi would cover her with animal skins inside the cave. Then he would climb to a higher point above their hideout to keep watch and to be sure the invaders did not harm her. There was no more time for talk. They must sleep. The cold fall air had settled into the cave, but there would be no fire tonight to warm them. The *saltu* were too close.

In the morning they heard them approach. Ishi and his cousin carried out their plan of survival. Elder Uncle leaned heavily on Ishi's cousin as she helped him across the rocky terrain to the swift waters of Deer Creek. A fallen alder tree was their bridge to safety. Ishi hoped the pile of animal skins that blanketed his mother would go unnoticed. Then he climbed to the rocky ledge high above their cave to watch.

He heard the men's excited voices as they discovered the three woven huts that made up their small campsite. Ishi watched as they carried out their belongings. Then they found the entrance to the cave. Ishi crawled to the edge of the rock above it and listened. The voices were softer and seemed to be speaking to his mother. Soon the men left carrying baskets and blankets and cutting their way back through the underbrush.

When Ishi could no longer hear their voices, he jumped down from the ledge and entered the cave. He gently picked up his mother and carried her underneath a circle of bay trees.

"They did not harm you?" asked Ishi tenderly.

"No, my son. They spoke softly to me and then left me alone." Her voice still held the fear of facing her enemy.

Ishi headed back to their village to gather what was left of their things. In the cookhouse he discovered that the fire drill, cooking utensils, and food were gone. He found only his mother's treasure bundle on a high shelf in the cave. Her feather cape, a bearskin cover, and some rabbit skin blankets were all gone. Ishi went to the *watugurwa*. His harpoon, knives, and chisels had been taken along with his bow, otterskin quiver, and his father's arrow. Emptiness filled him, and he felt helpless.

The following day two of the invaders returned to their hideout. Ishi watched them search the woven huts and wondered what else they could possibly take. One man placed a pocket knife and a sack of tobacco in the cave. Looking discouraged, the men headed back down the trail. By evening, Elder Uncle and Ishi's cousin had not returned to Deer Creek. Tomorrow he would go to look for them.

The next day, Ishi made his mother a comfortable bed of ferns by a feathery chamiso bush. He picked berries and left water in a small basket the raiders had overlooked. Then Ishi headed for Deer Creek.

The rains in the mountains had swelled the creek and strengthened the current. Ishi could see footprints in the sand on the shore. He crossed over the fallen log but could find no prints on the other side. Ishi quickly looked up and down the creek for signs of his family. He looked in the fishing shelter. The hooks, net, and harpoon were as he had left them. Ishi fought against the swirling waters as he swam in the river, searching for evidence of their whereabouts, or their bodies.

Tired from the struggle, Ishi dragged himself to the bank of the creek. A mountain wind pushed dark clouds over the sun and blew through the tall pines, singing to Ishi. He listened to the wind song of his ancestors sing the sad story of Three Knolls, Green Cave, and now, Deer Creek. Ishi wept.

It began to thunder. He hurried to the bay trees where he had left his mother. She was sleeping and her face looked soft and peaceful. He dreaded the words he would have to tell her once she awoke.

Again thunder came roaring into the canyon. Lightning blazed against the sky. Ishi carried his mother inside the cave.

There were no animal skin blankets to warm them and no fire drill to start a fire. Ishi gathered his frail mother in his arms and held her as if she were a child. In a hushed voice she asked about the lost ones. He told her of his desperate search for them and of the song the wind had sung to him. She weakly took his hand in hers and whispered that it was good he heard the song. The song would lead the lost ones to the trail of the dead. She begged her son to sing to her so she could go with them.

Ishi held his dying mother in his arms.

Ishi wrapped his arms around his mother. He sang of the Yahi canyon, of its deer and elk. He sang of the rushing rivers and the flowers in the meadows. Then his mother closed her eyes and died.

Ishi made a fire drill from a large piece of cedar bark and an oak stick. He dug out a small niche in the bark and placed the stick inside. Ishi surrounded the drill with dried grass for tinder. He twirled the stick in his hands until the grass smoldered and gave off a spark. Once a fire was made, Ishi mixed some of the ashes with pitch and painted mourning stripes across his face. With another stick he burned his hair close to his head to express the loss of his loved ones.

Ishi was the sole survivor of the Yahi Indians. For the next three years, he would not hear the sound of another's voice. He would not know the comfort of another's touch. Ishi would not know or ever have dreamed that the *saltu* would be the ones to rescue him from his life of solitude and starvation.

Finally, in August of 1911, a hungry and weary Yahi left his lonely hiding place and made his way to a slaughterhouse outside Oroville, California. He was looking for something to eat. Instead, he found a place in history.

# Chapter Six

## A Journey to Old Lands

Kroeber could not get Ishi's story out of his mind. The professor spent hours writing and rewriting the accounts Ishi had provided. Sleep did not come easy. At night he rolled and tossed in bed, reliving scenes of the Yahi scattering into the woods, tracked and trailed by white invaders. For forty years the Yahi had lived in fear and hiding, their numbers ever dwindling. And for three years Ishi had lived alone, speaking only to creatures of nature, without another person to share a meal or hunt or fish with. Kroeber felt ashamed and guilty for the pain his people had caused.

But there was guilt to be shared by the Yahi also. Not all the *saltu* slain were thieves and killers. Some were innocent settlers, drawn west by dreams of a better life. Did such people deserve to lose their tools and clothing, their food and livestock, even their lives to people they did not know? The question haunted

Kroeber. How could the Yahi and *saltu* ever forgive each other?

Despite the sadness Kroeber felt, he was certain of one thing. The professor was grateful Ishi had left his hiding place and ventured into Oroville. If he hadn't, the true story of his people and culture would never have been known. For three years Ishi had lived alone, with no other voice, no other living body with whom to share. It was no wonder that now he spoke so fast, even though he knew many did not understand his words.

The more Kroeber thought about Ishi, the stronger an idea grew in his mind. What if they returned to the places where the Yahi lived—Mill Creek and Deer Creek? Ishi had shared so much about the Yahi from his memory. Could he remember even more if he went back to the places of his past?

When Kroeber suggested the idea to Ishi, he was reluctant. After all, he had wanted to leave that world behind. It was one thing to tell about his past life; it was another to return to it. Ishi was troubled that by going back, he would disturb the eternal peaceful sleep of his people—or bother those souls still roaming the land. Beliefs about death were sacred to the Yahi. Ishi had seen the skulls of Native Americans the museum had in the back storeroom. He hated them. The Yahi felt the body should not be tampered with once the life had left.

But Kroeber was persistent. He enlisted Waterman's help too. They reminded Ishi of how grand it would be to go back to the fresh streams to catch fish, to hunt game, and to explore the mountainside caves. This time there would be no fear of the dreaded *saltu*. It would provide a chance to make sure the burial sites of his people were intact. "It would be a grand and glorious journey," Kroeber declared.

Another voice joined Kroeber and Waterman's in their quest to go back to the Yahi grounds. Dr. Saxton Pope taught at the University Medical School next door to the museum. He had given Ishi a medical examination and the two became friends. Ishi called his doctor friend "Popey" and taught him how to use a bow and arrow. In return, Dr. Pope invited Ishi to observe surgical operations. At first, the Indian was shocked at his friend's work with people's bodies. But the shock gradually became curiosity and then respect.

When Pope learned of Kroeber's idea to take Ishi back to Deer Creek country, he asked to go too. Confined to the antiseptic quarters of a hospital all year, Pope yearned for the outdoors, and camping with a Native American posed exciting possibilities. Pope also asked to bring his eleven-year-old son, Saxton Jr., along.

Finally, Ishi agreed. The bond of friendship had grown strong, and he saw the journey as a chance to repay those who had given him a new home. His trust in Chiep was complete. If the professor felt such a trip was good, it had to be true.

The group of five travelers attracted countless stares as they rode in an open Pullman drawing room car in May of 1914. Eyes widened at the variety of bow cases, quivers full of arrows, battered cooking pots, and specimen boxes that the group brought with them. Kroeber organized and reorganized all they had, wanting to make sure the trip was no disappointment.

It was an overnight jaunt from San Francisco to Vina, a town in the Deer Creek valley. Ishi slept in the upper berth of the car, smiling as he climbed the short ladder to his bed. His merriment continued the next morning when he tipped the surprised railway porter twenty-five cents as the group left the train. "He seems to be enjoying this adventure already," an amused Kroeber said to Waterman.

There seemed little doubt about that. When two hired guides joined the exhibition, it was clear Ishi felt they were not needed. This was his land, after all, and he knew this valley well. He was unaccustomed to riding a horse and clearly disliked the experience. He had hunted them before, but only for food when deer and salmon were scarce. But, if it was necessary to ride, then he would do so. Kroeber, Waterman, Pope, and his son were his friends. They had provided him food and shelter at their home. Now it was his turn to share.

In the days and weeks that followed, that is exactly what Ishi did—share. The group first made camp where Sulphur Creek flowed into Deer Creek. The water was clear and fresh, offering a perfect spot to bathe and play.

While swimming one afternoon, young Saxton Pope found himself slipping under the water, gasping for breath. Ishi sensed the boy's plight and swam to him quickly. Starting to thrash helplessly, Saxton Jr. grabbed Ishi's long hair and wrapped his hands into it. Ishi swam with Saxton Jr. under his arm with swift sure strokes to the shore. Once he had regained his senses, the boy shared the story with the others. They cheered Ishi, who simply smiled and nodded. That night, and many nights that followed, Ishi taught the boy the simple steps of the Yahi Circle Dance around the open campfire. Dr. Pope provided music with a ukelele.

Each day offered new chances to explore. Ishi's memory was alert as he and the two guides led the exhibition. The group surrounded Ishi as he carefully used an adze to make a strong bow from a firm piece of hickory. They watched his every move as he trimmed and shaped an arrow, then mounted a stone point. Silently the group waited as Ishi covered his mouth with his hand, then pulled it away, calling for rabbits. He then showed them how to shoot a rabbit while standing or kneeling.

The creeks proved another classroom for the visitors. With salmon abundant in the area streams, Ishi showed his friends the best means for catching the fish. He did not use fishhooks. Instead, Ishi assembled a double-pronged spear to a firm sheath. When a salmon came within view, he caught the fish between the two prongs. Quickly, he swooped the salmon in a net.

Kroeber constantly scribbled notes, not wanting to miss anything. This opportunity might never come again. What was written now would teach others.

Ishi did not plan every lesson. When a day of hunting failed to produce deer, Dr. Pope was disappointed. He was even more chagrined when Ishi suggested it might be caused by the doctor's habit of smoking tobacco. Ishi was convinced that deer were turned away by the smell of smoke lingering on a person's breath and body. A "No Smoking" rule was put into effect. Within two days, the group killed a deer.

When Kroeber and Pope brought a rattlesnake they had killed into camp, the reactions were mixed. Ishi did not hide his disgust. He believed that getting close enough to a rattlesnake to kill it was foolish. The thought of eating the creature was even more ridiculous! But Kroeber remembered someone saying that rattlesnake meat was much like frogs' legs—a delicacy. They sliced and fried the rattlesnake. Ishi wanted none of the meal, and Saxton Jr. and the two guides begged away from it too. But, the others took ample portions. The texture, they said, was tough and it tasted terrible. Kroeber noted that Ishi seemed to derive "much satisfaction from the results," displaying a wide grin as the men ate.

Although everyone in the group was a veteran camper accustomed to living in the wilderness, Ishi

was undoubtedly the neatest. Whether he was cleaning a fish or butchering a deer, his hands took surely
and carefully to the task. Not a speck of the catch was
wasted nor was the deerhide impaired. He never left
any scraps to attract flies or other insects. When Ishi
cooked, the food tasted better. Ishi modestly accepted
the compliments of his friends.

With each passing day, Professor Kroeber was
happier that they had made the trip back with Ishi. He
had learned the lessons of day-to-day survival—how
a bow was strung and a fish was caught—but better
than that, the anthropologist observed the feelings of
a Native American toward the land and water and sky.
Kroeber watched how Ishi cupped water in his hands
to drink, how he inspected soil, and how he stared at
the moon. There was something spiritual about Ishi's
motions, each movement seemed a prayer of thanks
to nature. Kroeber felt a deeper appreciation for so
much he had taken for granted. So did Waterman and
the Popes. Not only had Ishi shown his friends the
way he had lived, he had shared his love for that life
too. Despite the hardships he had endured, he still felt
close to the world that had fed him and given him
survival.

For years at the museum, Ishi had tried so hard to

Ishi showed his friends how to harpoon salmon in the rushing river.

share his story, to make strangers know from where he had come and what he had done. But without common language, it had been difficult, often impossible. Here, in his homeland, he could show them. He could show how to climb up and down a rope against sheer canyon walls, how to stalk a deer, or how to find shelter and warmth during a storm. In doing all these things, he could make a place for his people in history. He was the last of his tribe, the last Yahi who had grown up knowing only the old ways. Someday he too would venture into death and rejoin his ancestors. By showing how the Yahi lived, Ishi insured his people would not be forgotten. Kroeber sensed all of this.

As the professor filled page after page in his notebooks, Ishi drew map after map of villages and trails, hidden caves, and burial sites. Each spot had its own Yahi name, so priceless to the world of anthropology. Waterman took as many pictures as he could. Whether Ishi posed upright to loose an arrow or playfully swam in a freshwater stream, the moment was captured on film.

Each day they visited a new place: A shallow cave overhanging Mill Creek served as a refuge from pouring rains; a patch of plants and herbs that Ishi taught the others to use for food and medicine. Everything he taught them was compiled by Kroeber and Waterman in notes, maps, and photographs.

Finally, it was time to go back to the museum. Each member of the expedition knew that this had been a special time. Even as they talked about returning, the party knew the second time would never be the same.

The party was surprised when it arrived at Vina for the return trip to San Francisco. Curiosity seekers crowded the station, eager to see Ishi. He did not disappoint the audience. He shook hands, sang songs, and even knelt to demonstrate how to shoot a bow. But, when the train pulled into the Vina station, Ishi was the first of the group to get aboard. He seemed ready to leave.

With the sound of hissing steam and the rumbling of giant wheels, the train began slowly rolling along the track. Suddenly, there he was waving his hat and leaning out of a window. "Ladies and Genelemen!" Ishi yelled. "Good-bye!"

# Chapter Seven

---

## Final Sunset

Once back in the museum, Ishi returned to his caretaking duties with renewed energy. Now and then Kroeber mentioned someday returning to the Yahi spots, but Ishi showed little interest in another trip.

Ishi spent more time in his small room at the museum. He kept everything he owned in order. His clothes, tools, combs, and brushes rested neatly on a shelf or in a drawer. He wrapped gifts he received, including a scented bar of soap and a can of talcum powder, in paper. They were treasures to Ishi from caring friends, too precious to be used.

Ishi was as careful about his own appearance as he was his room and belongings. He bathed daily, a custom of the Yahi, and spent several minutes each morning combing his long, black hair. He then plucked his whiskers with tweezers made from split wood.

Visitors to the museum found Ishi totally at ease

and willing to talk. "He is a people person," wrote one reporter. "He speaks quickly, with broken words and phrases, but he is completely comfortable with strangers."

Ishi preferred being with people rather than by himself. With friends, he enjoyed being teased—and teasing right back. When he told a long story, he would raise his voice in excitement. If it was a humorous story, he was the first to laugh, his head nodding as if to show listeners how they should react.

Despite his enjoyment of people, Ishi still dreaded big crowds. When he had first arrived at the museum, he grew nervous in groups of five or six people. That fear had long passed. Showing his skills with a bow or singing old tribal songs made Ishi happy. But automobile rides into San Francisco, where he saw hundreds of people at one time, still left Ishi awestruck. Professor Kroeber attributed the reaction to the years of living with a tribe of four. "A lone American had always been a signal of imminent danger to him; no wonder that a hundred literally paralyzed him," wrote Kroeber.

Kroeber and Waterman strained to hear and understand every word Ishi spoke. Ishi, however, showed little interest in learning English. Once he understood enough words to use in day-to-day life, he did not want to learn more. He was fascinated by people's names, always asking Kroeber *"Achi djeyauna?"* or "What is his name?" upon meeting someone new. He also liked to know people's nationalities and professions. But he shied away from lengthy conversations that might drain his vocabulary. Ishi knew the power of his smile and his cheerful attitude, using them on everyone who came to the museum.

Ishi was the main attraction at the Museum of Anthropology. On one Sunday, over 1000 visitors poured onto the museum grounds. The most often asked question was "Where is Ishi?" Again and again, he patiently chipped out an arrowhead. Time after time, he bent his bow and sent an arrow zipping through the air.

Ishi noticed big changes taking place at the museum during the winter of 1915, his fifth year of living there. Never before was there so much painting and cleaning on the Berkeley campus and the hilly streets beyond. San Francisco was preparing for a major celebration. The Panama-Pacific International Exhibition was scheduled to begin on February 20. The event commemorated the opening of the Panama Canal. The canal made more direct shipping between the eastern and western United States possible.

One of the most dramatic displays in the center of the exhibition was a giant statue of a weary Native American seated on his downcast steed. Entitled "The End of the Trail," the plaque beneath the statue read "the drooping stormbeaten figure of the Indian on the spent pony symbolizes the end of the race which was once a mighty people." Americans no longer saw Native Americans as a threat or savages. They were simply a reminder of the past, a passing figure in the history of a growing nation.

As the last of his people, Ishi attracted much of the exhibition's spotlight. Invitations poured into the museum for him. Professor Kroeber wanted Ishi to choose what he wished to do at the celebration. The Great Northern Railway encouraged the Blackfoot tribe to invite Ishi to join them. It was a big publicity stunt, and at first, Ishi seemed willing. But once he understood that he would be giving up his own heritage and culture, he declined. He had lived a Yahi all this life—he would die a Yahi.

Despite the growing crowds that came to the museum on Sundays, Ishi gradually showed less interest in demonstrating his skills with a bow and arrow. The happy songs and chatter disappeared. He appeared more tired and spent more time lying down. A nagging cough plagued him. Yet he begged off being examined.

For years Professor Kroeber had been trying to gain the help of Edward Sapir, the world's greatest expert in Native American language. Perhaps Sapir could understand more of Ishi's dialect. Finally, in June of 1915, Sapir agreed to come. Kroeber decided to take a sabbatical to study in Europe, feeling such a trip would allow Sapir and Ishi to work more closely. Professor Waterman put Ishi up in his home, providing the best in good food, proper rest, and healthy recreation. Everyone hoped Ishi's cough would get better.

Morning, noon, and night, Ishi visited with Sapir. The noted linguist's ear picked up many of Ishi's words, and he wrote everything in notebooks. "It is exciting work, but exhausting," observed Sapir. Apparently, it was even more tiring for Ishi. After three months, he collapsed. He entered the University Hospital in San Francisco with Dr. Pope supervising examinations and tests on his patient and friend.

The diagnosis was not good. All signs pointed to tuberculosis. Despite research that was taking place, the disease frequently proved fatal.

Once his strength returned, Ishi left his own bed to visit others in the hospital. He helped the nurses clean instruments and moved from sickroom to sickroom, silently spending a few minutes in each. Patients seemed pleased to have him present. He made no sound, yet he conveyed a friendly attitude of concern with his smile and quiet demeanor. Sometimes he quietly hummed some of his favorite old tribal songs, the soft sounds bringing sleep to patients needing it most. "Your medicine is as valuable as mine," Dr. Pope told Ishi appreciatively. "Maybe even more."

In October of 1915, Ishi returned to the museum. A large sunny room was waiting for him that caught the fresh California breezes. An aide was assigned to keep a careful watch over Ishi, taking his temperature and keeping close records of his health.

Dr. Pope checked his patient often and kept Professor Kroeber informed by letter. Ishi seldom wanted to eat, and the food he took in seemed to distress him. He was most happy lying in bed and looking out his window at the ironworkers climbing the steel construction of the new hospital nearby. His eyes brightened, he would smile, and say, "All a same monkey-tee." The construction men climbed and dangled much like monkeys on the scaffolding.

Now and then the Ishi of the past returned, and he sought an audience. For hours he would talk about the old days, of making bows and hunting. He would make a few arrows, his slender reed-like fingers twisting and turning. He still managed to chip out a few arrowheads too.

There was little doubt that Ishi was weakening. The distress of eating became plain. Tears rolled down his narrowing cheeks as he tried to take in a few bites of food. Even water made him writhe in agony. He didn't complain. A Yahi was brave, willing to accept suffering. In life, Ishi had faced many dangers and suffered much. It would not be suitable for him to complain as he grew closer to the end.

One day Dr. Pope had an idea. Ishi enjoyed being photographed. Perhaps it might lift his spirits to have his picture taken. Dr. Pope also knew it might be the last chance for such an opportunity.

The two men posed for a photographer, Ishi and Dr. Pope each holding a bow, but the contrast was startling. Whereas Pope stood, firmly aiming his bow towards an imaginary target, Ishi sat below the physician, barely able to lift his lowered bow. Gone was the lean and muscular frame, the intense expression, the fiery eyes. Now there was nothing but a gaunt, shrunken frame, and a pained face. Dr. Pope regretted having taken the picture.

Despite his steadily weakening condition, Ishi occasionally rallied. His coughing lessened, his temperature dipped. He tried to speak, and for a moment, his face showed awareness of the world around, the people standing near who wanted to help.

But then it was gone. The cough returned. His skin burned with fever. He mumbled a request—"sweet water." He wanted spring water in place of the city water. The request was quickly granted.

Returning from Europe, Professor Kroeber went to New York to continue his research. He insisted on being kept closely informed about Ishi. As his friend's health continued to slip, Kroeber feared what might happen if Ishi should die. No doubt there would be those who would want an autopsy, an after-death operation to examine his body. As far as Kroeber was concerned, to autopsy Ishi served no purpose, and it violated one of Ishi's sacred beliefs about death.

Ishi's high temperatures and inability to eat convinced Professor Kroeber that death was near. He wanted his friend treated with respect and dignity, the way he had been treated from the first time he arrived at the museum. Tuberculosis had done its fatal job.

Certainly, if there could have been a way of saving Ishi, Pope would have found it.

Kroeber knew there would be doctors who would want to perform an autopsy out of curiosity. On March 24, 1916, he wrote a message to his friends at Berkeley in the event that Ishi should die:

> As to the disposal of the body, I must ask you as my personal representative on the spot in this matter, to yield nothing at all under any circumstances. If there is any talk about the interests of science, say for me that science can go to hell. We propose to stand by our friends.

Kroeber requested that everyone in the hospital who had helped Ishi be thanked. The professor directed his friends to purchase a plot for Ishi in one of the city's public cemeteries. Kroeber promised to take care of the financial details later.

While Kroeber's letter headed west, Ishi's condition worsened. Dr. Pope and others gathered around Ishi's bedside. The old man mumbled, different expressions appearing on his face. Perhaps his thoughts slipped through the wrinkles of time to when he was

At Ishi's death, a mask was made of his face.

a boy again. He stood in the shadows of his people, carving his first bow, sharpening arrowheads, catching salmon, and collecting acorns. He saw the early morning sun rise over mountaintops. He raced in the grass again, enjoying the fresh morning dew. Streams flowed freely, snaking paths down a mountainside. They were good days, those days so long ago, when a tribe lived together off the rich land. But always they watched, on guard against the approaching *saltu* who would attack and plunder.

Ishi's friends were caring and concerned. They eased his pain as much as they could, knowing their efforts could do little to stave the inevitable. Shortly after noon on March 25, 1916, Ishi died. It was the time of year when Deer and Mill Creeks boasted countless salmon on their annual spring run, when the clover and brushland sprouted new patches of green. As nature cycled to new life, a figure from the past departed.

Professor Kroeber's letter regarding Ishi's death was still in the mail when he died. An autopsy was performed and Ishi's brain was preserved.

Long before his death, Ishi had told Dr. Pope that the way to dispose of the dead was to burn their bodies. It was decided to place special momentoes in his coffin before his request would be honored. These included one of his bows, five steel pointed arrows, a basket of acorn meal, ten tusk shells, a box full of shell-bead money he had saved, a purse full of tobacco, three rings, and some obsidian flakes.

The coffin was cremated at the Mount Olive Cemetery in San Francisco. Ishi's ashes were placed into a small, black Pueblo jar. On the outside of the jar was inscribed: "Ishi, the last Yahi Indian, died March 25, 1916." The jar was placed in the columbarium at the cemetery located in the small town of Colma outside San Francisco. Later, in his room at the museum, $523 in cash was found, neatly arranged in a dresser drawer.

Newspapers carried the news of Ishi's death across the country. The account that appeared in the *Chico Record* of March 28, 1916 was bitter:

> "Ishi," the man primeval, is dead. He could not stand the rigors of civilization, and tuberculosis, that arch-enemy of those who live in the simplicity of nature and then abandon that life, claimed him. Ishi was supposed to be the last of a tribe that flourished in California long before the white men reached those

shores....He furnished amusements and study to the savants of California for a number of years, and doubtless much of Indian lore was learned from him, but we do not believe that he was the marvel that professors would have us believe. He was just a starved-out Indian from the wilds of Deer Creek, who, by hiding in its fastnesses, was able to escape the white man's pursuit. And the white man with his food and clothing and shelter finally killed the Indian just as effectually as he would have killed him with a rifle.

But most obituary accounts reflected sadness for the departed Indian. "Ishi was a link to our past," wrote one Midwestern newspaper editor. "With his death, that link is gone."

Dr. Pope felt his friend's lost deeply. He wrote,

And so, stoic and unafraid, departed the last wild Indian of America. He closes a chapter in history. He looked upon us as sophisticated children—smart, but not wise. We knew many things, and much that is false. He knew nature, which is always true. His were the qualities of character that last forever. He was kind; he had courage and self-restraint, and though all had been taken from him, there was no bitterness in his heart. His soul was that of a child, his mind that of a philosopher.

"He was the best friend I ever had in the world," Waterman wrote to Kroeber. Feeling he had pushed Ishi too hard during the summer of 1915 and weakened his friend, Waterman carried a deep sense of guilt for the rest of his life.

Kroeber, too, felt he had not watched over his friend carefully enough. For a time after Ishi's death, he gave up his profession of anthropology and studied psychoanalysis. Although encouraged by many to write Ishi's story, Kroeber refused. His wife, Theodora, compiled all the records and notes about Ishi, writing a manuscript she labeled as "a responsibility, not a pleasure."

In 1966, a monument to Ishi was dedicated outside Oroville, the town in which Ishi made his first public appearance in 1911. Nature lovers have also preserved an Ishi Wilderness in the region where Ishi was born and spent his early years.

# Timeline

**1848—Treaty of Guadelupe-Hidalgo.** The United States is proportioned lands from Mexico in present-day California, Arizona, New Mexico, and Texas. Much of the territory the United States acquired was Indian land.

**1853—First mass murder of Yahi.**

**1860-1865—Ishi is born.** Specific date is unknown.

**1861-1865—Civil War.** Clashes between Native Americans and whites intensify.

**1865—Three Knolls Massacre.**

**1872-1884—Twelve Year Concealment.** Ishi and thirteen others fled whites and survived hidden in the shrinking wilderness.

**1876—Alfred Louis Kroeber born.**

**1894—Sole Survivors**. Ishi, his mother, Elder Uncle, and a female cousin flee to Deer Creek until their discovery in October 1909.

**1909-1911—Ishi lives alone in the wilderness, the last of his people.**

**1911—Ishi arrives in Oroville.** August 29 he is discovered collapsed on the ground near a slaughterhouse.

—September 4 Ishi arrives at University of California at Berkeley.

**1914—Return to Banya Creek.** Ishi visits Yahi country with Kroeber, Waterman, and Pope in May.

**1916—Ishi dies.** On March 25, the last American Yahi died from tuberculosis.

# Glossary
## of Yahi Words

auna—fire
banya—deer
daana—baby
dambusa—gentle, pretty
dawana—wild
hansi—many
haxa—yes
hexaisa—leave
ishi—man
jupka—butterfly
kuwi—doctor
mahala—mother
mahde—sick
maliwal—wolf
marimi—woman
mudjaúpa—chief
saltu—white people
sigaga—quail
simini—pine wood
su—ah, well
suwa!—thus it is!

tetna—bear
Waganupa—Mt. Lassen
wakara—full moon
wanasi—hunter
watugurwa—men's house
wateree—quail
wowi—home
yana—human being
yuna—acorn

**Numbers:**
baiyu—one
uhmitsi—two
bulmitsi—three
daumi—four
djiman—five
baimami—six
uhmami—seven
bulmami—eight
daumima—nine
hadjad—ten

# Bibliography

Driver, Harold E. *Indians of North America*. Chicago: Un. of Chicago Press, 1961.

Franklin, Paula A., *Indians of North America*. New York: David McKay Company, Inc., 1979.

Heizer, Robert F., comp., *The Indians of California: A Critical Bibliography*. Bloomington: Indiana Un. Press, 1976.

Heizer, Robert F. and Theodora Kroeber, eds., *Ishi: The Last Yahi: A Documentary History*. Berkeley: Un. of California Press, 1979.

Josephy, Alvin M., Jr., ed., *American Heritage Book of Indians*. New York: American Heritage, 1961.

Kroeber, Theodora. *Ishi in Two Worlds: A Biography of the Last Wild Indian in North America*. Berkeley: Un. of California Press, 1961.

Kroeber, Theodora. *Ishi: Last of His Tribe*. Berkeley: Parnassus Press, 1964.

Malinowski, Sharon, ed., *Notable Native Americans*. New York: Gale Research, Inc., 1995.

Meyer, Kathleen Allan. *Ishi: The Story of an American Indian*. Minneapolis: Dillon Press, 1980.

Shorris, Earl. *The Death of the Great Spirit: An Elegy for the American Indian*. New York: Simon & Schuster, 1971.

Vogel, Virgil. *This Country Was Ours*. New York: Harper & Row, 1972.

# Sources

## CHAPTER ONE

p. 12, "The attire of the Indian..." Heizer, Robert F. and Kroeber, Theodora. *Ishi: The Last Yahi—A Documentary History*. Berkeley: University of California Press, 1979, p. 93.

p. 16, "wild man," Heizer and Kroeber, ibid., p. 8.

p. 19, "Wild Man of Oroville," Heizer and Kroeber, ibid., p. 128.

## CHAPTER TWO

p. 21, "Very well. He shall be..." Kroeber, Theodora. *Ishi In Two Worlds*. Berkeley: University of California Press, 1989, p. 128.

p. 24, "Tell him, Batwi, white man..." Heizer and Kroeber, op. cit., p. 99.

p. 26, "And sitting in the box you see..." Kroeber, op. cit., p. 140.

p. 27, "*Hansi, saltu*," Kroeber, ibid., p.139.

p. 28, "I should like to live here..." Kroeber, ibid., p. 218.

## CHAPTER THREE
p. 29, "Chiep," Kroeber, ibid., p. 124.

## CHAPTER SIX
p. 65, "Popey," Kroeber, ibid., p. 177.

p. 73, "Ladies and Genelmen! Good-bye!" Kroeber, ibid., p. 216.

## CHAPTER SEVEN
p. 76, "*Achi djeyauna*? What is his..." Kroeber, ibid., p. 135.

p. 79, "All a same monkey-tee." Kroeber, ibid., p. 243.

p. 81, "...sweet water," Heizer and Kroeber, op.cit., p. 236.

p. 82, "If there is any talk..." Kroeber, Theodora. *Alfred Kroeber—A Personal Configuration*. Berkeley: University of California Press, 1970, p. 92.

p. 85, "Ishi, the last Yahi Indian..." Kroeber, ibid., p. 246.

p. 85, "'Ishi,' the man primeval..." Heizer and Krober, op. cit., p. 242.

p. 86, "And so, stoic and unafraid..." Kroeber, op. cit., p. 248.

p. 87, "He was the best friend..." Kroeber, ibid., p. 245

# Index

0000113917520